** Please note it was not possible to include audio in every book format. If your book did not include any audio, you may download a **free** copy of these songs in MP3 format at SteveKaros.com*

ISBN-13: 978-1518713217

ISBN-10: 1518713211

Knock, knock.

Who's there?

Guitar.

Guitar who?

Guit-aren't you glad I didnt say ukulele!

Contents

Introduction

Why Is The Ukulele So Popular?

Over the years the ukulele has won the hearts of many people. It's size and portability make it easy to carry around and it's playability makes it a great instrument for beginners. This is not to say that only beginners should play the ukulele. There are many accomplished musicians that consider the ukulele their primary instrument.

"My Fingers Hurt"

As I look back at all the people I knew that started playing guitar, then promptly quit, I couldn't help but wonder how many of these people would still be playing music today had they started on the ukulele? Playability is an extremely important factor. If it's very uncomfortable to play your instrument, or if it hurts your fingers every time you play, chances are you will quit. Most ukuleles are quite playable and sound pretty good. Naturally you get what you pay for, but I've purchased ukuleles for around $30 and they were decent instruments all things considered.

"I Can't Read Music"

Learning to read music is important, it's a vital part of the arts. But for some people, time constraints make it very difficult to do so. Should these people be excluded from playing an instrument? Personally, I don't think so. Years ago, getting together and playing music was a natural pastime. Many of these people couldn't read music, many of them couldn't read at all! Once again, reading music is important, but it's not the only way to learn a song. Basic chord charts (which we use in this book), a playable instrument (any ukulele), and a little bit of time is all you really need. Music should be fun and easy to play, and that's what I love most about the ukulele... it makes music fun and easy to play!

Enjoy!

Steve

About the Songs

If a picture is worth a thousand words maybe a song is worth a thousand pictures? This is probably an exaggeration of course. Either way, I believe listening to the songs you are trying to learn is helpful.

The audio included with this book is very basic. Simple songs, from a simple guy. The recordings are just a reference. They are provided to give you an idea of what these songs **COULD** sound like, not what they **SHOULD** sound like. It's always important to interpret things your own way.

This book is not a substitute for a great teacher. I encourage all of you to take lessons if you can. This book is simply a guideline to help you get started on your journey. Something that will hopefully encourage you to start playing music... today, right here, right now!

Goodluck.

Parts of the Ukulele

There are different types of ukuleles but they all share the same basic characteristics

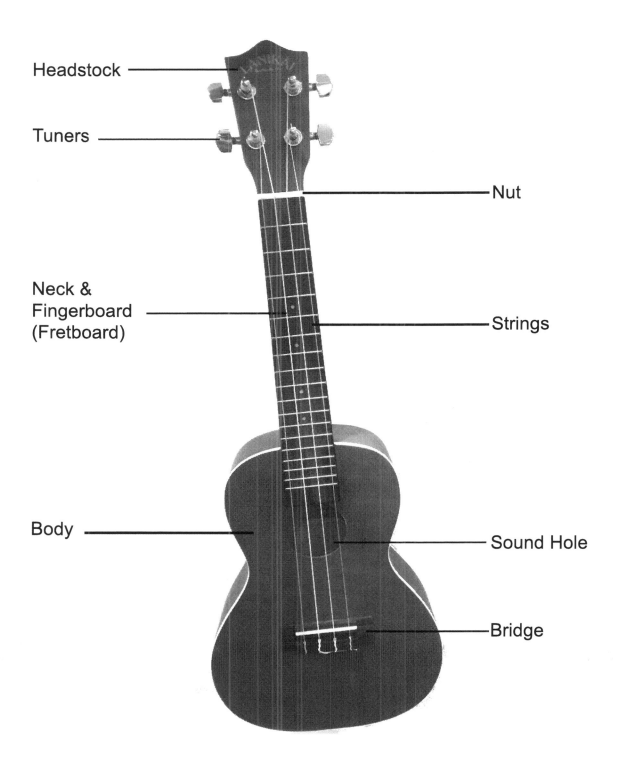

Headstock

Tuners

Nut

Neck & Fingerboard (Fretboard)

Strings

Body

Sound Hole

Bridge

Tuning the Ukulele

There are 4 strings on the ukulele. Usually the strings are tuned to :

G C E A

A great way to remember the names of the strings is a saying :

GOATS CAN EAT ANYTHING

G C E A

The strings are tuned from top to bottom, with the G string being on top.
Use a tuner, or match the pitch of the strings to another instrument. Remember to turn the tuning pegs slowly, a little goes a long way.

Fretting the Ukulele

"Fretting" is the term used for pressing the strings onto the neck of your ukulele. Usually your dominant hand is used to strum the strings and your other hand is used to "fret" the strings. For example, if you are right handed, you would strum with your right hand and fret with your left. Consequently if you are left handed you would strum with your left hand and fret with your right.

Strumming the Ukulele

Start by strumming the ukulele with your thumb or index finger. Later on you can experiment with using all your fingers, or a combination of fingers. The best place to strum is between the sound hole and the end of the fingerboard.

Basic Chords

A chord is simply a group of notes played together. To play a chord press each finger right behind the fret, the thin piece of metal that runs across the fingerboard. Press firmly and keep your thumb behind the neck of the ukulele.

The chords are represented in a diagram next to the picture. There will be similar diagrams located throughout this book.

C

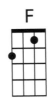

F

G

Strumming Patterns

A strumming pattern is the preset way in which we strum the strings of the ukulele. The ukulele is a very rhythmic instrument, and strumming it in different ways will give your music a different feel.

There is no right or wrong way to strum the ukulele. You can even strum the same exact song many different ways without actually changing the song. You can, and should, experiment with different strumming patterns to find the style that suits you best.

By sweeping our hands across the strings of the ukulele, in a combination of upward and downward strokes, we can create strumming patterns that give our songs a unique feel.

Listed below are just a few common examples.

Try these patterns with a C chord, and remember to briefly pause whenever you see the dash.

1st Strumming Pattern: **Down - Down - Down - Down**
2nd Strumming Pattern: **Down Up - Down Up - Down Up - Down Up**
3rd Strumming Pattern: **Down - Down Up - Down - Down Up**
4th Strumming Pattern: **Down - Down Up - Up Down**
5th Strumming Pattern: **Down - Down Up - Up Down Up**
6th Strumming Pattern: **Down - Down - Down Up Down Up**
7th Strumming Pattern: **Down - Down Up Down Up Down Up**

These are just a few basic examples. There are a lot of combinations when it comes to strumming patterns. Books have been written solely devoted to strumming patterns alone!

Songs for Beginners

These are one chord songs. They can be played by ringing out the chord and singing along, or by using a very basic strumming pattern.
(See the previous page for an example)

Are You Sleeping?

Are you sleeping? Are you sleeping?

Brother John, Brother John.

Morning bells are ringing, morning bells are ringing.

Ding ding dong, ding ding dong.

Row Your Boat

Row, row, row your boat, gently down the stream.

Merrily, merrily, merrily, merrily life is but a dream.

Tempo

The tempo is the speed of a song. We usually measure this speed in beats per minute. The higher the number is for the tempo, the faster the song will be. In this book the tempo will be listed near the title of the song.

Metronome

The tempo is used to give us a consistant time or rhythm as we play.
A great way to practice is by using a metronome. The metronome generates a steady beat that you can play along to. Start slow and select a speed you feel comfortable with.
Remember, everyone learns at their own pace.

Hush Little Baby

Traditional - tempo 110

Hush little baby don't say a word

Momma's gonna buy you a mocking bird

And if that mocking bird won't sing

Momma's gonna buy you a diamond ring

And if that diamond ring turns brass

Momma's gonna buy you a looking glass

(repeat chords with additional lyrics)

And if that looking glass gets broke, mommas going to buy you a billy goat.

And if that billy goat won't pull, mommas going to buy you a cart and bull.

And if that cart and bull turn over, mommas going to buy you a dog named rover.

And if that dog named rover won't bark, mommas going to buy you a horse and cart.

And if that horse and cart fall down, you'll still be the sweetest little baby in town.

He's Got The Whole World
In His Hands

Traditional - tempo 120

He's got the whole world in his hands, he's got the whole wide world in his hands.

He's got the whole world in his hands, he's got the whole wide world in his hands.

He's got the rivers and the mountains in his hands, he's got the hills and the oceans in his hands.

He's got the rivers and that mountains in his hands, he's got the whole world in his hands.

(Repeat chords with additional lyrics)

He's got the sun and the sky in his hands, he's got the moon and the stars in his hands.
He's got the sun and the sky in his hands, he's got the whole world in his hands.

He's got you and me brother in his hands, he's got you and me sister in his hands.
He's got you and me brother in his hands, he's got the whole world in his hands.

He's got the whole world in his hands, he's got the whole wide world in his hands.
He's got the whole world in his hands, he's got the whole world in his hands.

More Basic Chords

Below are some additional basic chords. Using minor chords and 7th chords will add texture and diversity to your music.

The pictures are just meant as a guideline. You can always experiment using different fingers to fret the chords.

Am

G7

 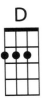

D

All Around The Kitchen

Traditional - tempo 144

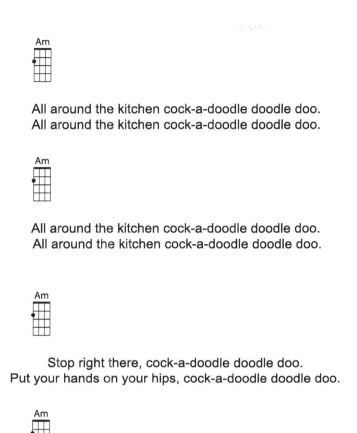

Am

All around the kitchen cock-a-doodle doodle doo.
All around the kitchen cock-a-doodle doodle doo.

Am

All around the kitchen cock-a-doodle doodle doo.
All around the kitchen cock-a-doodle doodle doo.

Am

Stop right there, cock-a-doodle doodle doo.
Put your hands on your hips, cock-a-doodle doodle doo.

Am

Let your body dip, cock-a-doodle doodle doo.
Spin around in a circle, cock-a-doodle doodle doo.

(repeat chords with additional lyrics)

All around the kitchen cock-a-doodle doodle doo. All around the kitchen cock-a-doodle doodle doo.
All around the kitchen cock-a-doodle doodle doo. All around the kitchen cock-a-doodle doodle doo.

Stop right there, cock-a-doodle doodle doo. Everybody freeze, cock-a-doodle doodle doo.
Wobble your knees, cock-a-doodle doodle doo. Waive your hands in the air, cock-a-doodle doodle doo.

All around the kitchen cock-a-doodle doodle doo. All around the kitchen cock-a-doodle doodle doo.
All around the kitchen cock-a-doodle doodle doo. All around the kitchen cock-a-doodle doodle doo.

Stop right there, cock-a-doodle doodle doo. Wiggle your nose, cock-a-doodle doodle doo.
Touch your toes, cock-a-doodle doodle doo. Spin around in a circle, cock-a-doodle doodle doo.

Stop right there, cock-a-doodle doodle doo. Put your hands in the air, cock-a-doodle doodle doo.
Like you just don't care, cock-a-doodle doodle doo. Spin around in a circle, cock-a-doodle doodle doo.

Tingalayo

Traditional - tempo 124

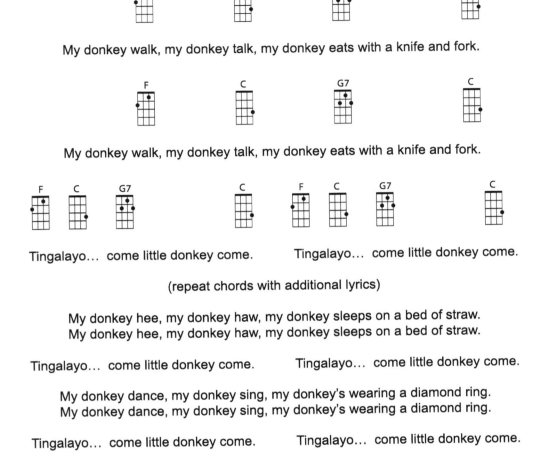

My donkey walk, my donkey talk, my donkey eats with a knife and fork.

My donkey walk, my donkey talk, my donkey eats with a knife and fork.

Tingalayo… come little donkey come.   Tingalayo… come little donkey come.

(repeat chords with additional lyrics)

My donkey hee, my donkey haw, my donkey sleeps on a bed of straw.
My donkey hee, my donkey haw, my donkey sleeps on a bed of straw.

Tingalayo… come little donkey come.   Tingalayo… come little donkey come.

My donkey dance, my donkey sing, my donkey's wearing a diamond ring.
My donkey dance, my donkey sing, my donkey's wearing a diamond ring.

Tingalayo… come little donkey come.   Tingalayo… come little donkey come.

Jingle Bells

Words & Music James L.Pierpont - tempo 134

G   **C**   **D**   **G**

Dashing through the snow, in a one horse open sleigh. O'er the fields we go, laughing all the way.

G   **C**   **D**   **G**

Bells on bobtail ring, making spirits bright. What fun it is to ride and sing a sleighing song tonight.

G   **C**   **G**   **D**

Jingle bells, jingle bells, jingle all the way. Oh what fun it is to ride in a one horse open sleigh.

G   **C**   **G**   **D**   **G**

Jingle bells, jingle bells, jingle all the way. Oh what fun it is to ride in a one horse open sleigh.

(repeat chords with additional lyrics)

A day or two ago, I thought I'd take a ride.
And soon Miss Fannie Bright, was seated by my side.
The horse was lean and lank, misfortune seemed his lot.
He got into a drifted bank and we got upshot.

Jingle bells, jingle bells, jingle all the way. Oh what fun it is to ride in a one horse open sleigh.
Jingle bells, jingle bells, jingle all the way. Oh what fun it is to ride in a one horse open sleigh.

A day or two ago, the story I must tell.
I went out on the snow and on my back I fell.
A gent was riding by, in a one-horse open sleigh.
He laughed as there I sprawling lie, but quickly drove away.

Jingle bells, jingle bells, jingle all the way. Oh what fun it is to ride in a one horse open sleigh.
Jingle bells, jingle bells, jingle all the way. Oh what fun it is to ride in a one horse open sleigh.

Now the ground is white, go it while you're young.
Take the girls tonight, and sing this sleighing song.
Just get a bobtailed bay, two forty is his speed.
Hitch him to an open sleigh and crack! You'll take the lead.

Easy Breezy Ukulele - SteveKaros.com

Folk Songs & Traditional Music

A folk song is usually passed down by oral tradition. Years ago, most people did not know how to read or write music. In those days a song had to be taught to another person in order for it to be handed down from one generation to the next. The original authors of most of these songs were not known. Through the years many of these songs have changed. Melodies have been altered, lyrics have been added and taken away.

In this book, folk songs are indicated by the term "Traditional" near the title. Feel free to change these songs to suit your own particular culture and taste.

Down By The Bay

Traditional - tempo 125

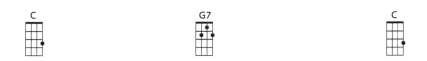

Down by the bay, where the watermelons grow, back to my home, I dare not go

For if I do, my mother would say…

Have you ever seen a crab haling a cab ? Down by the bay

(Repeat chords with additional lyrics)

Down by the bay, where the watermelons grow, back to my home, I dare not go
For if I do, my mother would say…
Have you ever seen a:

Dinosaur that couldn't roar
A cow pulling a plow
A snake baking a cake
Ants with polka dot pants

Or make up any rhyme you want !

Polly Wolly Doodle

Traditional - tempo 160

I went down south to see my gal polly wolly doodle all the day.

Oh my Sal, she's a spunky gal, polly wolly doodle all the day.

Fare thee well, fare thee well, fare thee well my fairy fay.

I'm going to Louisiana, to see my Susyanna, polly wolly doodle all the day.

(repeat chords with additional lyrics)

Oh my Sal, she's a maiden fair, polly wolly doodle all the day.
Curly eyes, laughing hair, polly wolly doodle all the day.

Fare thee well, fare thee well, fare thee well my fairy fay.
I'm going to Louisiana, to see my Susyana, polly wolly doodle all the day.

Oh my Jack, in a pumpkin patch, polly wolly doodle all the day.
Doing jumping jacks off a monkey's back, polly wolly doodle all the day.

Fare thee well, fare thee well, fare thee well my fairy fay.
I'm going to Louisiana, to see my Susyana, polly wolly doodle all the day.

I've got a friend named Bill, he won't sit still, polly wolly doodle all the day.
Singing do-si-do in a rodeo, polly wolly doodle all the day.

Fare thee well, fare thee well, fare thee well my fairy fay.
I'm going to Louisiana, to see my Susyana, polly wolly doodle all the day.

Chicken Grease

Words & Music Steve Karos - tempo 144

F   C   F   C

With a big old smile its the way I like to start my day. If you feel a little down I'll wipe your blues away.

F   C   F   C

I'll pick up my guitar, I'm heading on down the street. Singing a happy song to everybody I meet

C

Love, peace, chicken grease, these kinds of things sound good to me.

F   C   G   F   C

Oh well, you never can tell.   Oh well, you never can tell.

(repeat chords for 2nd verse and chorus)

I'm packing up my bags, I know that its time to go. I hit the road far away on a traveling show.
And all the kids that I meet listen to that rock n roll. I pick up my guitar and we all start singing along.

Love, peace, chicken grease, these kinds of things sound good to me.
I like blue skies, apple pies, I'm not the kind of guy that likes to cry.
Oh well, you never can tell. Oh well, you never can tell.

(Bridge)

F   C

I want to swing like a monkey through the trees. Fly sky high like a bumble bee.

F   D   G

Act real cool like a summer breeze. Come on everybody and sing with me.

Additional Chords

A few of these chords are a little more difficult to play. We use 4 fingers to fret the E minor chord, and this will require a bit of dexterity.
The B minor chord requires you to fret or "barre" 3 strings at the same time with your index finger. A barre chord simply means we're pressing down multiple strings with one finger. This will require you to build up some strength in your hands.
These chords may take a little more time to master, but don't get discouraged.

Em

Bm

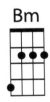

A

Water Comes To My Eye

Traditional - tempo 132

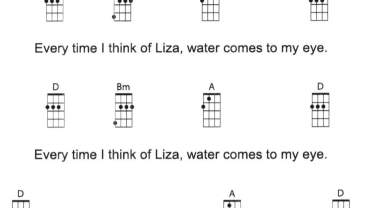

Every time I think of Liza, water comes to my eye.

Every time I think of Liza, water comes to my eye.

Come back Liza, Come back girl, the water comes to my eye.

Come back Liza, Come back girl, the water comes to my eye.

(repeat chords with additional lyrics)

Sit at home and wait for Liza, water comes to my eye.
My heart is sore but I wait for Liza, water comes to my eye.

Come back Liza, Come back girl, the water comes to my eye.
Come back Liza, Come back girl, the water comes to my eye.

When there's love, the time goes fast, water comes to my eye.
Time goes slow, when love has past, water comes to my eye.

Come back Liza, Come back girl, the water comes to my eye.
Come back Liza, Come back girl, the water comes to my eye.

This Little Light Of Mine

Traditional - tempo 126

This little light of mine, I'm going to let it shine.

This little light of mine, I'm going to let it shine.

This little light of mine, I'm going to let it shine.

Let it shine, let it shine, let it shine.

(Repeat chords with additional lyrics)

No one's going to put it out, I'm going to let it shine
No one's going to put it out, I'm going to let it shine.
No one's going to put it out, I'm going to let it shine.
Let it shine, let shine, let it shine.

Hide it under a bushel, no, I'm going to let it shine.
Hide it under bushel, no, I'm going to let it shine.
Hide it under a bushel, no, I'm going to let it shine.
Let it shine, let it shine, let it shine.

Oh! Susanna

Words & Music Stephen Foster - tempo 126

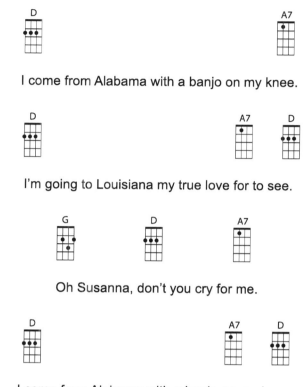

I come from Alabama with a banjo on my knee.

I'm going to Louisiana my true love for to see.

Oh Susanna, don't you cry for me.

I come from Alabama with a banjo on my knee.

(repeat chords with additional lyrics)

It rained so hard the day I left, the weather it was dry.
The sun so hot I nearly froze, Susanna don't you cry.

Oh Susanna, don't you cry for me.
I come from Alabama with a banjo on my knee.

I had a dream the other night when everything was still.
I dream I saw Susanna, coming down that hill.

Oh Susanna, don't you cry for me
I come from Alabama with a banjo on my knee.

The Hawaiian D7

A great chord to add to your vocabulary. Although it is not a "real" D7 chord, the Hawaiian D7 is easier to fret than a D chord and has a pleasantly distinctive sound. Sometimes, you can use this chord instead of a traditional D or D7 chord. For example, you can try and substitute the Hawaiian D7 for a D chord in the following song Midnight Special.

Hawaiian

D 7

Midnight Special

Traditional - tempo 120

C   **G**   **A7** **D**   **G**

You wake up in the morning, hear the prison bell ring. Go marching to the table…and its the same old thing.

C   **G**   **A7** **D**   **G**

It's on the table, nothings in your pan. Say anything about it …and your in trouble with the man

G   **C**   **G**

Let the midnight special, shine its light on me..

G   **A7**   **D**   **G**

Let the midnight special shine its ever-loving light on me.

G   **A7**   **D**   **G**

Let the midnight special shine its ever-loving light on me.

(repeat chords with additional lyrics)

If you ever come to Houston, you better walk right. You better not stumble and you better not fight.
Cause the sheriff will arrest you. He'll carry you down. Bet your bottom dollar, you'll be sugar land bound.

Let the midnight special, shine its light on me. Let the midnight special shine its ever-loving light on me.

Thelma told me that she loved me, I believe she told a lie. She hasn't been to see me, since last July.
She could've sent a little coffee, she could've sent a little tea. She could've sent me nearly anything, even the jailhouse key.

Let the midnight special, shine its light on me. Let the midnight special shine its ever-loving light on me.

Yonder come miss Rosie, how in the world do you know? I can tell her by her apron, and the clothes that she wore.
Umbrella on her shoulder, a piece of paper in her hand. I heard her tell the captain, I want to see my man.

Let the midnight special, shine its light on me. Let the midnight special shine its ever-loving light on me.

The biscuits on the table, there as hard as a rock. If you ever try and eat them, they'll break a convicts heart.
My momma sent a letter, my sister sent a card. If you ever want to see us, you're going to have to ride the rod.

Let the midnight special, shine its light on me. Let the midnight special shine its ever-loving light on me.

Easy Breezy Ukulele - SteveKaros.com

Beautiful Day

Words & Music Steve Karos - tempo 144

G   C   G   D   G

I wake up early in the morning everyday by eight. I gotta get myself to school I want to graduate.

G   C   G   D   G

Momma tells the teacher all the things that I want to be. I'm going to do it all momma, come on take a look at me.

G   D   G

I'm going to be a doctor, a lawyer, a teacher, I'll be on TV.

G   D   G   C

I'm going to be a fireman, the president, an astronaut, I'll be in the movies.

D   C   G   D   C   G

It's a beautiful day, a beautiful day to be me.   It's a beautiful day, a beautiful day to be me.

(repeat chords for 2nd verse and chorus with additional lyrics below)

I've got to study hard, I want to get the best of grades. If I'm going to make the dean's list I've got to get all straight A's.
Telling all my friends all the things that I want to be. I'm going to do it all friends come and take a look at me.

I'm going to be a scientist, a chemist, a biologist, I'll go on safari.
I'm going to be a singer, an actor, a dancer, I'll be on Broadway.

It's a beautiful day, a beautiful day to be me. A beautiful day, a beautiful day to be me.

(Bridge)

Em   D   C   G   Em   D   C

It's a great big world, step outside and see all there is to see. Find yourself and you can be what you want to be.

Everyday Superhero

Words & Music Steve Karos & Dan Siegler - tempo 132

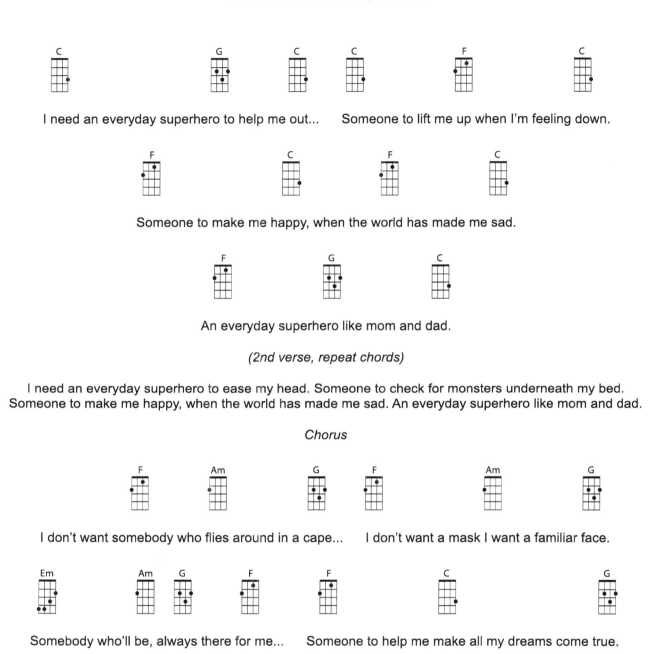

I need an everyday superhero to help me out...   Someone to lift me up when I'm feeling down.

Someone to make me happy, when the world has made me sad.

An everyday superhero like mom and dad.

(2nd verse, repeat chords)

I need an everyday superhero to ease my head. Someone to check for monsters underneath my bed.
Someone to make me happy, when the world has made me sad. An everyday superhero like mom and dad.

Chorus

I don't want somebody who flies around in a cape...   I don't want a mask I want a familiar face.

Somebody who'll be, always there for me...   Someone to help me make all my dreams come true.

(additional lyrics, repeat chords)

I need an everyday superhero to pull me through.
Someone to tolerate the crazy things I do.
Someone to make it right, when everythings gone wrong.
An everyday superhero like dad and mom.

I don't want somebody who flies around in a cape.
I don't want a mask, I want a familiar face.
Somebody who'll be, always around for me.
Someone to help me make all the pieces fit.

Ukulele Chord Chart

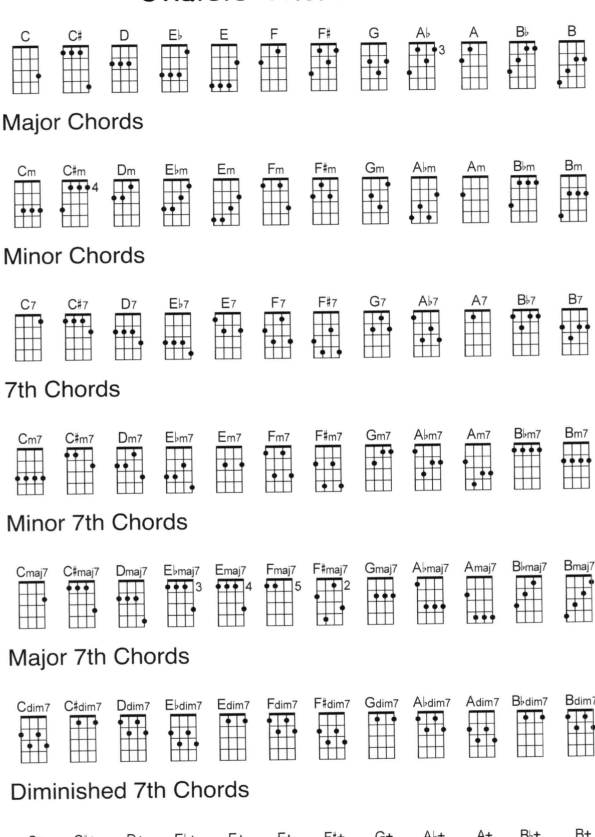

Conclusion

Congratulations! If you've made it this far, I hope the ukulele has become a daily part of your life. I highly encourage you to pursue your musical education with a qualified teacher. I also recommend playing with other people as often as possible. Music is a social experience. I firmly believe that sharing your music will make you a better player, musician, artist and overall person.

I hope this book and these songs played a small part in your musical progression. The world will always be a better place with more music in it, especially yours.

Steve Karos

Easy Breezy Ukulele

Songs

Are You Sleeping?
Row Your Boat
Hush Little Baby
He's Got The Whole World In His Hands
All Around The Kitchen
Tingalayo
Jingle Bells
Down By The Bay
Polly Wolly Doodle
Chicken Grease
Water Comes To My Eye
This Little Light Of Mine
Oh! Susanna
Midnight Special
Beautiful Day
Everyday Superhero

Printed in Great Britain
by Amazon